Who Was
E. B. White?

by Gail Herman

illustrated by Dede Putra

Penguin Workshop

To Amy and Maria, for all the times I talked
too much about E. B. White—GH

PENGUIN WORKSHOP
An imprint of Penguin Random House LLC, New York

First published in the United States of America by Penguin Workshop,
an imprint of Penguin Random House LLC, New York, 2022

Visit us online at penguinrandomhouse.com.

Library of Congress Cataloging-in-Publication Data is available.

Printed in the United States of America

ISBN 9780593386729 (paperback)   10 9 8 7 6 5 4 3 2 1 WOR
ISBN 9780593386736 (library binding)   10 9 8 7 6 5 4 3 2 1 WOR

Contents

Who Was E. B. White? 1

Young Elwyn 6

Trouble in School 15

Finding His Place 24

On the Road 30

A New Yorker 39

Life at *The New Yorker* 46

Changes and More Changes 58

Moving Out, Moving Back 64

The Mouse Is Out 74

Andy Takes a Stand 81

Spinning a Tale 88

Maine Events 96

Timelines 106

Bibliography 108

Who Was E. B. White?

It was spring 1926. E. B. White was riding an overnight train on his way home from Virginia's Shenandoah Valley to New York City. The initials in his name stood for Elwyn Brooks. But practically everyone E. B. White knew called him by his college nickname, "Andy."

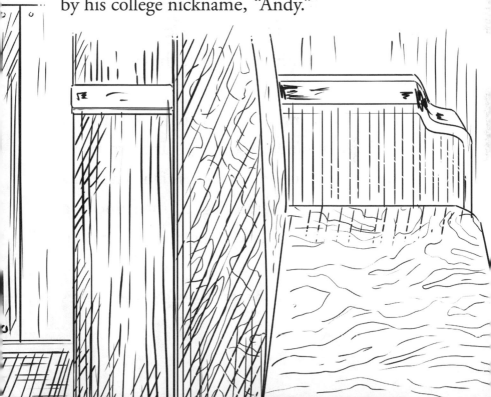

That night Andy dreamed about a brave mouse who was nicely dressed and carried a cane. He didn't know it yet, but the mouse was the inspiration for his first children's book.

At the time, Andy was twenty-seven years old. He was already a writer for newspapers and magazines. The idea of writing a children's book never crossed his mind. But Andy had always liked mice. When he was a child, at home and sick in bed, he met a pleasant house mouse. The mouse became a pet, and Andy even built it a home, complete with a gym where he could teach it tricks.

Andy wrote down every detail of the dream. He called the mouse Stuart. He started to make up adventures about Stuart for his eighteen nieces and nephews. They often begged their uncle to tell them stories. But he'd struggled to come up with ideas.

Twelve years later, he tried to get the stories

published. But an editor said no. So Andy put the stories in a drawer and went on to write other things. But he didn't forget about Stuart. Seven more years passed. Finally, he sent his stories to a different editor. That editor loved them.

In 1945, *Stuart Little* became a book—and a best seller! In time, E. B. White would write two other children's classics: *Charlotte's Web* and *The Trumpet of the Swan*.

At times, Andy still struggled with his writing. He never thought it was easy. But he couldn't imagine *not* writing.

For E. B. White, putting thoughts on paper was always his way to make sense of the world.

CHAPTER 1
Young Elwyn

Elwyn Brooks White was born over one hundred years ago, in 1899. Andy always said he was lucky, and it started with his birth. The date was July 11, or 7/11—two numbers thought to bring good fortune.

Back then, people didn't have radios or TVs. There were few cars. Big families were common. Andy had three older sisters and two older brothers. He was the "baby" of the White family. He joked that his mother had run out of names by the time he was born. Growing up, he was called En for short. He didn't like his real name, or the shortened one.

A 1920s family listening to the radio

The White family lived in a big comfortable house in Mount Vernon, New York. There were ponds, woods, and hills in Andy's neighborhood. Most families had stables or a barn, where they kept horses for riding.

It was only a half-hour train ride from Mount Vernon to New York City. Andy liked family visits there. All in all, he thought he had the best of both worlds.

Andy's father, Samuel, was the head of a piano company. Music filled the Whites' home. The six children were "practically a ready-made band," Andy explained in an introduction to one of his books. "All we lacked was talent."

At times, Andy felt lonely. His sisters and brothers were too old to play with him. But Andy had his imagination to engage him and the great outdoors to explore. He hiked through the woods. He rode his bike everywhere. Andy loved going wherever he pleased and seeing nature up close. He brought home lizards and turtles, snakes and rabbits. Sometimes he felt closer to animals than to people.

One day, Samuel brought home fifty eggs. He put them in an incubator, a big device that gave off heat so the eggs could hatch. Young Andy had to stand on tiptoe to see anything at all.

Once the eggs began to crack, tiny beaks poked through! He never forgot those baby chicks—or the importance of a simple egg, holding life.

When Andy was about five years old, he started to suffer from allergies. "Douse his head in cold water every morning before breakfast," one doctor said. But that odd advice didn't help. Instead, Samuel decided to take the family to Maine for the summer. He believed the fresh air would do Andy good.

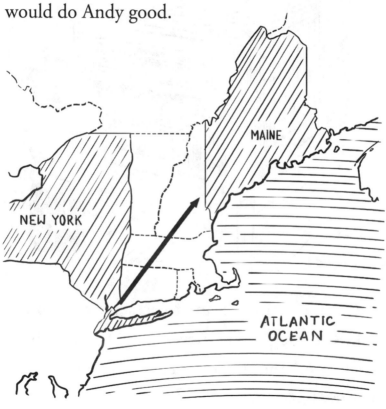

The Whites stayed in a cabin they called Happy Days. It was on Great Pond in central Maine. Everyone loved it there, but no one loved it more than Andy.

The family returned year after year. In Maine, Andy grew close with his brother Stanley. (He was eight years older, and he was called Bun or Bunny because he could wiggle his nose like a rabbit.) Stanley showed Andy how to paddle a canoe in a straight line. Together they studied wildlife.

Those summers meant the world to Andy. And after he started first grade in September 1905, the memories became even sweeter.

CHAPTER 2
Trouble in School

Andy was a worrier, even when he was young: "As a child I was frightened but not unhappy," he said in a 1969 magazine interview. "I lacked for nothing except confidence."

In first grade, Andy was already ahead in reading. That's not surprising since the Whites were a word-loving family. Stan taught Andy how to sound out words from the newspaper.

His other brother, Albert, kept a big dictionary in his bedroom. Their father sent all the children there when they didn't know a word. At dinner, Samuel recited limericks—funny five-line poems. Everyone tried to come up with a rhyming word for the end of the last line.

Andy was smart, but he didn't like school. He didn't like being stuck inside. Even worse,

he dreaded the assembly at the start of each day. The principal would call a different student up to the stage to read aloud. The principal went in alphabetical order.

The idea of speaking in front of all the students scared Andy. Luckily, *White* was at the end of the list. Still, one day "Elwyn White" was called to the stage. He had to read a poem that had the line

"Footprints on the sands of time." But instead, Andy said, "the tands of sime." Everyone laughed—at least it seemed that way to Andy.

Because of those assemblies, for the rest of his life, Andy stayed away from big events—even award ceremonies honoring him. He hated to be the center of attention.

Each school day, though, did have a bright side. His sister Marion had given him a dog, a collie named Mac. For six years, Mac met Andy on his way home. According to Andy, it was Mac's idea.

Through the years, Andy would have many, many dogs. They kept him company at every stage of his life. But in an essay called "Dog Training," Andy called Mac "the noblest, the best, and the most important. . . . When I got him he was what I badly needed."

Writing helped Andy, too. It made him feel better to write down his fears. He always liked stringing words together to make a sentence. It brought him joy.

When Andy was about eight, he began to keep a journal—and he wrote in it every day for the next twenty years. In the journal, he'd ask questions like, How does a bird know how to build a nest? and, What will I be when I grow up? He was already worried about the future. Andy kept writing. When he was nine, he wrote a poem about a mouse getting caught in a trap. The poem won a prize in a magazine. But Andy decided he didn't like it much. He never wanted to see a mouse get hurt. He sent stories to a magazine for young readers and won two prizes. Both were about dogs.

In 1913, Andy started high school. He was small for his age. He wasn't a star player on the football team, or even *on* any team. He refused to

go to school dances. Girls scared him.

Writing helped him through high school, too. He had pieces published in his school's literary magazine. But in his journal he wrote: "Eighteen, and still no future!" Andy could be very hard on himself.

Cornell University

World War I started in 1914, involving many countries in Europe and beyond. In April 1917, the United States entered the war. Short and skinny Andy didn't weigh enough to join the army. So in the fall, he left Mount Vernon for Cornell University in upstate New York. It was the same college Stan and Albert had attended.

Andy had always wanted to go there. But he had a rocky start at Cornell, too.

CHAPTER 3
Finding His Place

Andy arrived at Cornell before most students. Right away he had a misunderstanding with a man who worked at the college. Andy felt so awful he packed his bags. He wanted to go home. Then he calmed down and decided to stay.

Soon life at Cornell improved. It started with his name. The first president of the university was named Andrew Dickson White. At Cornell, anyone who had the same last name was immediately called Andy, too. And that was fine by Elwyn Brooks!

Unlike his experience in high school, Andy soon found his place at Cornell. He joined a fraternity—a club for college boys—and later became its president. He even got to bring his dog—a mutt named Mutt—to live in the frat house.

As a freshman, Andy started to work on the school's newspaper. *The Cornell Daily Sun* was considered one of the best college papers in the country. Andy paid more attention to working on the *Sun* than he did to classes. He wrote news stories, poems, and humor pieces. Anything that was needed. By his junior year, he was editor in chief.

Although he enjoyed writing, Andy wasn't much of a reader. He liked boating magazines more than great literature. But one of his English courses made a big impression on him. It was a grammar class taught by William Strunk Jr.

William Strunk Jr.

The professor was in a club whose members shared their own writing. Andy joined it. He was feeling more confident now. By senior year, he even had a girlfriend. He made up a funny name and wrote a poem about her that was printed in

the *Sun*. The poem was funny, too. He compared his girlfriend's eyes to Mutt's. To Andy, that was a big compliment.

Then came graduation. What would come next?

CHAPTER 4
On the Road

After college, Andy went home to Mount Vernon. He wasn't sure what career would suit him; he knew only that he liked writing. So in March 1922, he decided to take a road trip. He and his Cornell friend Howard "Cush" Cushman were going to drive across the United States. Maybe different places would give him ideas for what to write about—and maybe ideas for his future, too.

Andy had a car. It was a Model T Ford that he called Hotspur.

Driving cross-country was unusual back in 1922. There were few road maps. There were no highways connecting one state to another. Cush didn't even know how to drive. And the two friends didn't have much money. It wouldn't be easy. But the challenges didn't stop them.

Andy and Cush packed camping gear, two typewriters, a dictionary, a harmonica, and not much else. They set out from Andy's family home on March 9, heading west.

The Model T

The Model T (people called it the Tin Lizzie) came out in October 1908. After producing eight different car models (all with hand cranks to start them), company founder Henry Ford used the best parts of each to design the Model T. It wasn't the first car to run on gasoline. But it became the most popular one. Average Americans could afford the car. The price was low because so many could be made quickly. Ford was able to do this by creating an assembly line in his Detroit factory. A conveyor belt slowly went past a long line of autoworkers. Each worker added on one part to the car, which then moved further along the assembly line, with the next worker adding on the next part. Finally, there would be a complete car. Assembly lines produced thousands of cars a day. The last Model Ts were made in 1927. But the car remains important in American history. Due to its popularity, gas stations were built along more and more roads. Suddenly, people were driving everywhere!

Along the way to the West Coast, they stayed with friends and found odd jobs to make some money. At one stop, they sandpapered a dance floor and ran a carnival booth.

Still, money was tight. When Hotspur got a flat tire, Andy had to walk thirty-two miles so he could sell one of their typewriters to pay for a new one.

The friends had more car trouble when they reached the West Coast. Not far from Spokane, Washington, Andy and Cush drove up a steep ramp to board a ferry. But something in the car's engine snapped. The car slid backward.

Luckily, the ferry captain knew all about cars and fixed Hotspur.

Finally, after six months on the road, Andy and Cush made it to Seattle. But Cush was out of money. He left for home. Andy, however, rented a room and took a job at the *Seattle Times* in September 1922. He didn't like reporting on news events. So he began writing stories and poems for the paper. He liked that much better. But unfortunately, he lost the job in June 1923.

What was his next move? Spending all his money on a cruise to Alaska—a first-class one-way ticket! Andy had no idea how he would get back.

Luck was on Andy's side. The ship's captain offered him a job. If he worked in the bar, the return trip would be free. Andy thought it was all a lot of fun.

By then, Andy had been away eighteen months. When he got back home, he wanted to write about his adventures. He thought they might make interesting magazine pieces.

Eventually, they did. One of his most famous pieces—"Farewell, My Lovely!"—was about the Model T, plus Hotspur and the ferry.

Finally, Andy had found the right subject to write about—life as he saw it.

CHAPTER 5
A New Yorker

One afternoon in February 1925, Andy was at Grand Central Terminal, heading home to Mount Vernon from his job at an advertising agency in New York City. He stopped at a newsstand and spotted a brand-new magazine. It was called *The New Yorker*.

Andy liked the magazine right away. It had news articles. But it also had essays, poetry, and short stories. The tone was casual and funny, just the way Andy liked to write.

Andy decided to send in samples of his work. It didn't take long for the editors to recognize his talent. Soon they were publishing articles by him regularly.

The New Yorker

The magazine was founded in 1925 by Harold W. Ross, who had dropped out of school after tenth grade, and his wife, Jane Grant, a *New York Times* reporter. Ross wanted to create a new kind of magazine that was funny and aimed at worldly New Yorkers. He called it *The New Yorker*. It became known for publishing writers who'd go on to become famous. *The*  *New Yorker* drew readers from throughout the United States. Today, it remains one of the most influential magazines in the world.

Jane Grant and Harold Ross

In the summer of 1925, Andy made another decision: to quit his advertising job. He wanted to live in New York City and work as a full-time freelance writer. That meant he wouldn't be getting a weekly paycheck. He would get paid only if he sold a story or poem. It was exciting but scary, too.

Andy shared an apartment with three friends
from college. They lived in Greenwich Village, a
neighborhood filled with artists and writers. After
his friends left for work each morning, Andy
tidied up the apartment. He took long walks. He
was searching for topics to write about.

In December 1925, one of his *New Yorker* stories got a lot of attention. It was based on his own experience, about a man who goes to a diner where the server spills buttermilk all over his suit.

Andy saw that people liked reading about his own funny misfortunes. Well, that was something he could easily do!

Not long after that piece was published, the fiction editor at *The New Yorker*, Katharine Sergeant Angell, asked Andy to work full-time for the magazine. But Andy said no! He didn't want to be stuck in an office. It was the same way he'd felt in elementary school. But in 1926, he agreed to work for the magazine part-time. And for those days, yes, he agreed to work in the office.

It would change Andy's life.

CHAPTER 6
Life at *The New Yorker*

Andy began writing short articles, poems, captions for cartoons, and funny little pieces called newsbreaks. (When an article in *The New Yorker* doesn't quite fill a whole page, a newsbreak fills the empty space.) Andy would take a sentence or two from another magazine or newspaper article. Then he'd add to that, turning it into a joke.

One time he used a question a reader had sent to another magazine: "Dear Sir: What does it take to be a successful businessman?" the reader asked. Andy's answer: "A successful business."

It didn't take long for Andy to start working at *The New Yorker* full-time. He wrote the way he talked, in a modest, funny way. He never took himself too seriously. Sometimes he "interviewed" animals. In one piece, he asked a sparrow why he lived in a city and not in the country. (The reason: People dropped more food in a city.)

Soon *The New Yorker* became a big part of his life.

Andy shared an office with another writer. James Thurber was a humor writer, too. He was loud and chatty. Andy was quiet and shy. But they became great friends. They even worked on a book together. And Thurber, too, would go on to write famous children's books. They both became great friends with the fiction editor Katharine Sergeant Angell, who had hired Andy.

Katharine's marriage was ending. After she and her husband divorced, her friendship with Andy began to change. One morning in November 1929, Andy walked into Katharine's apartment. They talked about potted plants. The conversation wasn't anything special. Still, right then and there he "decided she was the girl for me." Kay, as he called Katharine, agreed! So they got married that day! Katharine's dog Daisy came along to the church. Daisy got into a tussle with the minister's dog. Andy later said, "It was a very nice wedding. Nobody threw anything and there was a dog fight."

James Thurber (1894–1961)

Thurber grew up in Columbus, Ohio, the middle child in a family with three boys. At seven, he lost an eye when his older brother accidentally shot him with a rubber-tipped arrow while they were playing. Thurber wore a fake eye for the rest of his life, but it never held him back. Eventually, he became a reporter. When he joined *The New Yorker*, Thurber became famous for his cartoons, many of which featured dogs. His works include plays and dozens of books. Some, including *The 13 Clocks* and *Many Moons*, are books for children.

Katharine Sergeant Angell White (1892–1977)

Katharine was born in Winchester, Massachusetts, the youngest of three daughters in a well-to-do family. Always intent on having a career—unusual at the time—she attended Bryn Mawr College. Not long 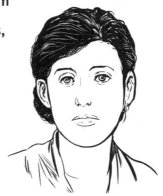 after graduating, she married her first husband, attorney Ernest Angell. Eventually the couple settled in New York City. At age thirty-two, with two young children, Katharine started part-time work as a manuscript reader at *The New Yorker*. Within months, she was the full-time fiction editor. She shaped the literature printed by the magazine—discovering many authors, such as J. D. Salinger and John Updike.

The next day, it was business as usual. Andy and Katharine were back at work. But that didn't take away from their happiness. Andy called marrying Katharine "the most beautiful decision" of his life.

Katharine's children, twelve-year-old Nancy and nine-year-old Roger, lived with their father during the week and with Katharine and Andy on weekends. Soon Andy grew close to them.

One cold winter morning on a trip to Boston, Andy took Roger skating on a frozen lake in the Public Garden. They hid their shoes under a bush. Andy's were gone by the time they finished. He had to walk along busy city streets, still wearing skates. People stared.

Andy never liked attracting attention. But he enjoyed making fun of himself. And he wanted to turn it into a fun adventure for Roger. To make him laugh, Andy got into a racing position and called himself The Skater. It worked.

To Roger, Andy didn't seem like most grown-ups. He had "a readiness for play . . . ," Roger said later, "that lasted all his life."

Meanwhile, *The New Yorker* was thriving. As one of its star writers, Andy was famous. Collections of his magazine pieces were published as books. His first, *The Lady is Cold: Poems by E.B.W.*, came out in 1929. (The title poem was about a statue in a fountain outside a fancy New York City hotel.)

By 1930, the United States was deep into the Great Depression, a period of hardship with millions of people out of work. Andy and Katharine, however, were very fortunate. They didn't have to worry about money.

On December 21, 1930, Andy and Katharine's son, Joel, was born. With a growing family, Andy wanted a home in a place he loved: Maine. It had always been a dream of his. It was time to make that dream come true.

The Great Depression

During the 1920s, there was a business boom. Many people throughout the United States invested money in stocks, which are shares of ownership in companies. But the boom years didn't last. Companies began to lose money, and when the stock market crashed in October 1929, the stocks became

worthless. People lost money, all their savings for many. Factories and businesses closed. Farms were wiped out. By 1932, one in every four adults was out of work. Hundreds of thousands were homeless. Millions went hungry. The Great Depression spread throughout the world, ending with the start of World War II in 1939, when wartime needs demanded more workers, factories, and products.

CHAPTER 7
Changes and More Changes

In 1933, the Whites bought a farm. It was on the Maine coast in a town called North Brooklin. They planned to spend time there but also keep their apartment in the city.

The White family farm

Meanwhile, the Great Depression dragged on around the world. Some countries' governments were changing. In Europe, dictatorships—meaning that one leader has absolute power—were on the rise. The dictator in Germany was Adolf Hitler.

Andy was deeply worried about world events, especially in Europe. He began to write more political pieces. He spoke up for democracy, and for protecting people's rights around the world. But was he making a difference? Andy didn't know.

He worried about his health, too. He was having stomach problems, fevers, and dizzy spells. He took the deaths of his father and mother, in 1935 and 1936, very hard. Maybe, he thought, all that stress was causing his health problems. Struggling with worry and depression would continue from time to time through the rest of his life.

In 1937, Andy decided to take time off from *The New Yorker*. The leave would be temporary, he said, while he figured things out. He called the hiatus "My Year."

Adolf Hitler and the Nazis

Adolf Hitler and his Nazi political party led Germany from 1933 to 1945. They believed in dictatorship, not democracy, and that a proud, powerful Germany had the right to rule other countries. Hitler also wanted to wipe out all Jews. In Germany and in countries that Nazi troops invaded, Hitler took basic rights away from Jewish people; he then forced them and citizens from certain other groups into prison camps and, after that, death camps. About six million Jews perished in what came to be known as the Holocaust, along with millions of others.

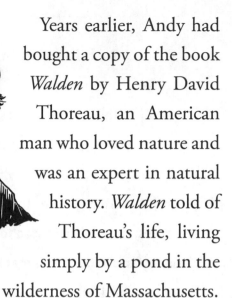

Henry David Thoreau

Years earlier, Andy had bought a copy of the book *Walden* by Henry David Thoreau, an American man who loved nature and was an expert in natural history. *Walden* told of Thoreau's life, living simply by a pond in the wilderness of Massachusetts.

The book had been so important to Andy, he carried it everywhere.

Andy understood the need for living close to nature. *His* "year," he decided, would be spent in Maine. He'd live like Thoreau had—on his own—while Katharine and six-year-old Joel stayed in New York.

CHAPTER 8
Moving Out, Moving Back

Andy's "year" lasted only eight months. He missed his family too much to be away from them for longer. Katharine knew, however, that his heart was in Brooklin. So in 1938, she agreed to give up their New York City apartment. Maine was where the Whites would live year-round.

Seven-year-old Joel took to life in rural Maine right away. He loved going to the two-room schoolhouse and living near the water. The move was more difficult for Katharine. She had planned to continue at *The New Yorker*. But working remotely back then was nearly impossible. So Katharine gave up her editor position at the magazine.

Andy, too, gave up most of his work at *The New Yorker*. In 1937, he began writing a column for *Harper's Magazine*. The publication came

out once a month, not every week like *The New Yorker*. He'd have more time to dig a little deeper into whatever subject he was writing about.

Andy called the column "One Man's Meat." In it, he spoke his mind. Sometimes about world issues.

In 1939, for example, World War II broke out in Europe after the Nazis invaded Poland.

Andy thought the United States should take a bigger role, raising its powerful voice against Hitler. War was necessary, he believed, to "fight for the things which Nazism seeks to destroy."

Not everyone in the United States agreed with Andy. In September 1940, a large political group called the America First Committee formed to oppose joining the war.

That same month, Andy wrote a *Harper's* column simply titled "Freedom." He said, "The

Europe before World War II

least a man can do at such a time [as this] is to declare himself and tell where he stands. I believe in freedom."

America First Committee

The powerful group—it had eight hundred thousand members at one point—was against the United States fighting the Nazis, believing that America's interests came first, even if it meant Germany won the war and Hitler remained as its dictator. The committee disbanded after enemy planes bombed Pearl Harbor in Hawaii on December 7, 1941.

After the December 7, 1941, attack on a US military base in Pearl Harbor, the US joined England, France, and other countries to fight against Germany and its allies.

Attack on Pearl Harbor

Weeks later, Andy traveled to Washington, DC, to help write a pamphlet. The pamphlet was based on a now-famous speech by President Franklin D. Roosevelt called the "Four Freedoms." It was about the importance of democracy. The US government wanted people to read more about President Roosevelt's ideas—what a free, just, and peaceful world could look like after World War II.

Andy wanted to do more to help FDR's vision become reality. In Maine, he served as a plane spotter. He raced up and down dark roads at night, looking for enemy airplanes. He had a horn to blow to warn of any danger. (Fortunately, the mainland of the United States was never attacked.) *Am I doing enough?* Andy asked himself.

Joel, twelve years old, was leaving home for boarding school. And because of the war, *The New Yorker* didn't have enough staff to put out a weekly magazine. Andy wanted to help there, too.

Roosevelt and the "Four Freedoms"

On January 6, 1941, when many Americans still thought the United States should stay out of World War II, President Franklin D. Roosevelt gave an important speech to Congress. In it, he outlined why Americans should support the war effort. He believed the United States should help win freedom for people around the world. He spoke about freedom of speech,

Franklin Delano Roosevelt

freedom of worship, freedom from want (poverty), and freedom from fear. Roosevelt's speech was so powerful, the United Nations still uses its principles to protect human rights.

There was more of a reason to go back to New York City and less of one to stay in Maine. Katharine was thrilled. She could work, once again, at the magazine she loved. But of course, they'd still keep the farm in Maine. Andy wouldn't want it any other way.

Andy resigned from *Harper's Magazine* in March 1943. He returned to *The New Yorker*, hoping to "help tidy up the world."

CHAPTER 9
The Mouse Is Out

The war . . . the state of the world . . . leaving the farm. It was a lot to handle. Too much in fact for Andy. He had what he called "a nervous crack-up" in 1943. He felt like his head had "a kite caught in the branches somewhere." He said that he felt so odd, he thought he might die.

Andy saw many doctors. Eventually, he felt better. But Andy worried that time was running out. He was determined to finish the stories he'd started back in 1926 about the little mouse, Stuart.

Even though many years earlier, an editor had rejected the Stuart stories, Andy had kept the pages in a drawer. He had never forgotten about his adventurous mouse. "It must be a lot of fun to write for children," he wrote in 1938, in his *Harper's* column, "One Man's Meat."

Anne Carroll Moore was a very important children's librarian at the time. She was also a devoted fan of Andy's magazine column. She encouraged him to write a book for children. She didn't know Andy had already written some stories about Stuart.

Anne Carroll Moore

Andy thanked her. Then, two weeks later, he sent his Stuart pages to the editor of his adult books. "The story," Andy told him, "would seem to be for children, but I'm not fussy who reads it." The editor was excited. He asked Andy to keep writing. But for Andy, there was always something else to do. Once, he explained, he was busy tending 250 chicks.

More years passed without much more written. Then, at age forty-five, thinking he might die during his nervous breakdown, Andy finally sat down at his typewriter. Stuart's adventures were about boating and canoeing, skating and exploring—all the things Andy loved doing. And like Andy, Stuart was small with a big-sized spirit of fun.

It was early 1945. So much time had passed, Andy had a new editor, Ursula Nordstrom. She was head of the Department of Books for Boys and Girls at Harper & Row. Just before the book was printed, she sent a copy of the story to Anne Carroll Moore, who had encouraged him to write a children's book. But after reading all about

Stuart, Moore told a friend, "I was never so disappointed in a book in my life." She couldn't understand how a mouselike child could be part of a human family. Was it fantasy? Or was it supposed to be reality?

Andy didn't think there had to be rules for a story. Or that a book had to be one thing or the other. He respected children. He had faith they'd understand.

Stuart Little was published in October 1945.

Moore had retired years earlier from the New York Public Library. But she was still important in  the field of children's literature. She made her opinion known across the country. *Stuart Little* was banned by many libraries.

Children and Libraries

Before the late 1800s, most US public libraries didn't allow children younger than fourteen to have library cards—or even to step inside the building. But after a study published by the US Bureau of Education in 1876 said it was important for children to have books available for free, librarians took notice. In 1887, the Pawtucket Public Library in Rhode Island became one of the first to create a separate space for children, roping off a corner of its reading room. In 1890, the public library in Brookline, Massachusetts, opened a true children's room—in the basement—mainly to keep noisy kids out of the adult sections. There was no librarian; the building janitor was in charge. When a library in Pasadena, California, opened a children's room in 1900, children had to hold out their hands, to show they were clean, before they could touch a book.

But thanks to the important New York City librarian Anne Carroll Moore, today almost every library has its own children's room and librarians, many with play areas, story times, crafts, comfy chairs, and lots of books.

Maybe I made a mistake, Andy thought. *Maybe the book should never have been published.* Then thousands of letters from children started pouring into the publisher's office. Kids loved the story. *Stuart Little* sold more than one hundred thousand copies in one year.

Andy had been right all along.

CHAPTER 10
Andy Takes a Stand

By 1945—the year *Stuart Little* was published—it was clear that World War II was ending. That meant the end of Germany under Nazism. Once the war was over, there would be a new world order. Andy was terribly interested in what it would be like. That spring, he traveled to San Francisco to write about an international conference. Representatives from fifty countries were coming together to form the United Nations, a new organization dedicated to world peace.

Andy wrote about the group's progress. But he'd already taken the idea further. To end all wars, he thought, there should be *one* world government. Every country on the planet would be under one flag, with the same basic freedoms for everyone.

His pieces were collected in the 1946 book *The Wild Flag*. Andy didn't think he was going to convince anyone. He just wanted to tell people

his ideas. He never pretended to be an expert. He strived to be "a reliable man." Someone people could trust to be truthful.

In the 1950s, Andy saw dangers right at home in the

United States. A senator from Wisconsin, Joseph McCarthy, started to investigate Americans who might belong to the Communist political party. In Communist countries, people don't have the right to own land or businesses. The government owns everything. It has all the power. People also don't have the right to express beliefs the government doesn't like.

In a democracy, such as the United States, everybody has these rights and more. Andy believed the McCarthy investigations in Congress went completely against the idea of democracy.

In a letter to a New York newspaper, Andy wrote: "Like other Americans, my acts and my words are open to inspection—not my thoughts or my political affiliation." (*Affiliation* means being associated with or connected to a particular group, such as a political party.) What Andy meant was, there are laws that prevent Americans from doing some things. But the US government has no business saying what a person can believe.

To Andy, it was part of the freedoms he held dear.

Andy spoke up for civil rights also—for equality no matter a person's race. He wrote pieces against segregation—the idea that Black people should be kept apart from white people. He supported the Civil Rights Act of 1964, which made segregation and discrimination against the law. Andy said it was "morally right."

What else did Andy care about? The planet itself.

Way back in 1927, Andy first wrote about pollution. In 1959 and 1960 alone, Andy published seventeen columns on the environment in *The New Yorker*. That's why a woman named Rachel Carson got in touch with Andy. She suggested he write an article about the danger of pesticides, chemicals sprayed on crops and farm animals to rid them of certain types of insects.

Andy said no. He agreed it was an important issue. But he wasn't a scientist. Rachel Carson was. He told Carson *she* should write it. She did. *The New Yorker* ran her pieces beginning in June 1962. The articles turned into *Silent Spring*, a book that inspired the environmental movement.

Rachel Carson

The environment, civil rights, democracy, and freedom—those issues, and Andy's words about them, are as important today as they were decades ago. The proof is that as recently as 2019, a new collection of Andy's political writings came out, *E. B. White on Democracy*. His personal take on life, too, is still meaningful. In 2020, another book was published, featuring Andy's letters: *Chickens, Gin, and a Maine Friendship: The Correspondence of E. B. White and Edmund Ware Smith*.

Meanwhile, in the late 1940s, Andy was settling in to work on another children's book. He began spinning a tale about a spider.

CHAPTER 11
Spinning a Tale

In the fall of 1947, one of Andy's pigs died. Andy had tried hard to save this pig. Nothing worked. Andy, however, realized there was a way he could save another pig—one that was in a children's book.

But what would the story be? he wondered.

One year passed without an answer. Then Andy noticed a spider in his barn. She was always busy, spinning new strands. Her web was a thing of beauty. Andy was fascinated.

The spider began spinning a sac. She was getting ready to lay eggs. Andy brought over a stepladder for a closer look. The spider was elegant, he thought, gray and brown with striped legs.

Andy never saw the spider again. But the web and the sac remained. A few days later, Andy put the sac in a candy box filled with air holes and took it all the way to his New York apartment. Soon enough, hundreds of tiny spiders climbed through the holes. They strung webs across Andy's dresser.

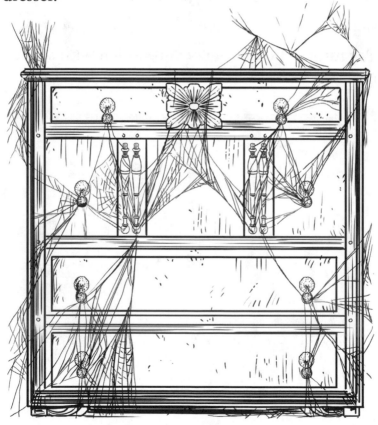

Andy watched, still fascinated. Even after the spiders left, he kept thinking about them—and their mother. Then he had it! The mother spider would be the hero of his pig story! And the spider's babies could figure into it, too.

Andy spent an entire year studying spiders. The story would have talking animals. But he wanted it to be as true to nature as possible.

Finally, Andy was ready to write about Wilbur the pig and Charlotte the spider. He wanted to tell a tale of friendship. On the Arable family farm, pigs eventually are killed for their meat. But Charlotte works to save Wilbur's life, by weaving words into her web praising the young pig. Andy wanted to portray life on a farm, too—its beauty and hard truths, and nature itself. He wanted to get everything exactly right.

Spiders and Charlotte

Spiders are scientifically classified as arachnids—not insects. There are about forty thousand species, and they all have eight legs and eight eyes, with no antennae or wings. Almost all are predators, using their superstrong silk thread to catch prey. Charlotte in *Charlotte's Web* is a common barn spider and orb weaver, spinning spiderwebs that look like wheels. Trapdoor spiders burrow into the ground, where they build a trapdoor of dirt, plants, and silk. The spiders

Orb weaver spider

scuttle out, to surprise a passing insect. Hammock spiders hide inside webs that look like hammocks while they wait for prey. The black widow spider is considered one of the most dangerous spiders in North America, with a bite that can cause severe pain to humans. Its web may look like a messy tangle, but it's really a carefully thought-out trap.

Andy finished the first draft on January 19, 1951. Then he spent another year revising.

Finally, he surprised Ursula Nordstrom, his editor, at her office. "I've brought you a new manuscript," he said, holding out the only copy of *Charlotte's Web*.

In 1953, *Charlotte's Web* won a Newbery Honor, a top award in children's books. It went on to become one of the most popular books in children's literature—ever.

How Popular Is *Charlotte's Web*?

A modern classic, *Charlotte's Web* still tops best-seller lists decades after it was published. *Publishers Weekly*, a magazine about the book-publishing business, has called it the best-selling children's paperback ever. When PBS came out with its *Great American Read* TV series in 2018—a national survey of the one hundred most-loved novels ever published—it was number seven. The book inspired three movies. The first, an animated film, came out in 1973, followed by *Charlotte's Web 2: Wilbur's Great Adventure*, also animated, in 2003. By the time a live-action movie hit theaters in 2006, *Charlotte's Web* had sold forty-five million copies. It has been translated into at least thirty-five languages. And it's still going strong today!

CHAPTER 12
Maine Events

Four years passed. Andy was now fifty-eight and Katharine was sixty-five. She was ready to give up her full-time work as fiction editor. Again, they decided to live in Maine year-round.

At last the time was right.

Andy was happy to be in Maine. He had lots of time for farming. He was writing as he pleased.

His next book turned out to be very different from any of the others.

A college friend had sent Andy a gift, a little-known book about grammar written by Andy's old English professor, William Strunk Jr. *The Elements of Style* stated that all writing should be clear and brief. "Omit needless words," Strunk always said.

The professor had died years earlier. To honor his memory, Andy wrote about Strunk and his book in a 1957 *New Yorker* column. A publishing company decided to bring out a new edition of *The Elements of Style*. Andy's essay became its introduction. In fact, Andy revised the entire book and added a brand-new chapter.

The new edition came out in November 1959. It became a best seller—plus required reading for high-school and college students.

Now the "little book," as Strunk had called it, was big. Thanks to E. B. White.

In Maine, time passed happily. Joel owned a boatyard and lived close by. Andy and Katharine spent lots of time with all their children and grandchildren.

But by 1968, both Andy and Katharine were facing serious health problems. Katharine needed a lot of medical care. And that made Andy worry. Did they have enough money to pay for it all?

Luckily, Andy had an idea for a project that could help pay the bills. A new children's book.

A while earlier, Andy had read a newspaper article about trumpeter swans. Trumpeters are known for their musical calls. The news article made Andy wonder: What if a trumpeter swan was born without a voice? Maybe it would use an actual trumpet instead. And just like that, Andy had the plot for *The Trumpet of the Swan.*

This book, he decided, would have adventure *and* a love story. It would feature Louis—a swan named after famous trumpet player Louis Armstrong—and a swan named Serena.

Just months later, Andy sent the manuscript to Ursula Nordstrom, his editor. "If you think the book is promising, let me know," he wrote in November 1969. "And if you think it's lousy, I would like to know that too."

The book came out the very next year. Andy
had another best seller.

Trumpeter Swans

Graceful and elegant, the trumpeter swan is the largest waterbird in North America and one of the heaviest flying birds in the world. With a wingspan of ten feet, it needs a lot of open water— just about the length of a football field—for takeoff.

From the 1600s to the 1800s, trumpeters were hunted for their feathers, skin, meat, and eggs. Their habitats were harmed by pollution and land development. By 1932, there were fewer than seventy trumpeters worldwide. To protect the swans from extinction, strict hunting laws were passed and environmental cleanups began. Today, trumpeters number in the tens of thousands.

These were special but difficult years for the Whites. Katharine's health declined. In July 1977, she was rushed to the hospital. Andy stayed by her side, holding her hand. Her heart slowed, then stopped on July 20.

The great love of Andy's life was gone. He couldn't bear to go to the funeral. So he wrote a piece about Katharine, to be read out loud. And in a letter to a friend, he wrote: "I don't know what I ever did to deserve a wife with Katharine's qualities, but I have always had a lot of luck."

Five years later, in 1982, Andy handed in his final piece for *The New Yorker*. It was a newsbreak. Altogether, he'd written some thirty thousand of them.

His own health was failing by then. But Andy made the best of things. He played with his grandchildren and tinkered around the farm. He traveled a bit. He even rode his bicycle till just about his eighty-fifth birthday.

In August 1984, Andy went on a canoe trip. When he tried to lower the canoe from the car roof, it slipped, hitting him on the head. That night, he felt confused. Over the next few months, the confusion grew worse. Doctors thought the accident caused the problem.

Soon Andy was spending all his time resting. Joel visited every day. He read to him, often from Andy's own work. Sometimes Andy asked Joel who wrote those pieces. "You did, Dad," Joel would say. And Andy would reply, "Well, not bad."

Andy's writings were, in fact, greatly admired. Over the years, he won award after award, including, in 1963, the Presidential Medal of Freedom, the highest honor a US civilian can receive. (A civilian is someone who isn't in the military.) In his children's books and his magazine pieces,

Presidential Medal of Freedom

Andy proved he was a friend to all—an author who cared deeply about the world and its living things.

At age eighty-six, on October 1, 1985, Andy died at his beloved Maine farm. "It is not often," he wrote at the end of *Charlotte's Web*, "that someone comes along who is a true friend and a good writer."

Like Charlotte, E. B. White was both.

Timeline of E. B. White's Life

1899 — Elwyn Brooks White is born on July 11 in Mount Vernon, New York

1905 — Spends his first summer in Maine

1913 — At fourteen, wins a gold badge in a magazine writing contest for "A True Dog Story"

1917 — Goes to Cornell University and is nicknamed Andy

1922 — Begins his cross-country adventure on March 9

1926 — After submitting pieces to *The New Yorker*, accepts an office job at the magazine

1929 — Marries Katharine Sergeant Angell

1930 — Son Joel is born

1933 — Buys a farm in Maine

1937 — Starts writing the "One Man's Meat" column for *Harper's Magazine*, work that will continue for five years

1945 — *Stuart Little* is published

1952 — *Charlotte's Web* is published

1957 — Moves to Maine to live year-round

1963 — Awarded the Presidential Medal of Freedom

1970 — *The Trumpet of the Swan* is published

1982 — Fully resigns from *The New Yorker*

1985 — Dies on October 1 at age eighty-six

Timeline of the World

1899 — German company Bayer patents aspirin

1913 — The first crossword puzzle appears in a New York newspaper

1917 — The United States enters World War I on April 6

1929 — President Herbert Hoover has the first telephone installed in the Oval Office

1930 — Colonel Harland Sanders, founder of Kentucky Fried Chicken, opens his first restaurant

1933 — Construction begins on San Francisco's Golden Gate Bridge

1937 — Future president Ronald Reagan makes his acting debut in the movie *Love Is on the Air*

1952 — Sainted humanitarian Mother Teresa opens her first home to help the sick, dying, and poor of Calcutta, India

1963 — President John F. Kennedy is assassinated on November 22, in Dallas, Texas

1982 — US computer scientist Scott E. Fahlman creates the first computer emoticon: a "smiley face" made of punctuation marks

1985 — A catastrophic earthquake in Mexico City on September 19 leaves more than 10,000 people dead, tens of thousands injured, and 250,000 homeless

Bibliography

*Books for young readers

Elledge, Scott. *E. B. White: A Biography*. New York: W. W. Norton & Company, 1984.

Guth, Dorothy Lobrano, editor. Revised and updated by Martha White. *Letters of E. B. White, Revised Edition*. New York: HarperCollins Publishers, 2006.

*LaBrie, Aimee. *Who Wrote That? E. B. White*. Philadelphia: Chelsea House Publishers, 2005.

Sims, Michael. *The Story of Charlotte's Web: E. B. White's Eccentric Life in Nature and the Birth of an American Classic*. New York: Walker & Company, 2011.

*Sweet, Melissa. *Some Writer! The Story of E. B. White*. Boston, New York: Houghton Mifflin Harcourt, 2016.

White, Martha, editor. *E. B. White on Democracy*. New York: HarperCollins Publishers, 2019.